Inhale slowly...
exhale slowly!

Focus your
mind!

Stay in
the present!

Allow yourself
to feel!

Focus on
your breath!

Notice what
you feel!

If your mind wanders
focus on coloring!

Inhale 4s
hold 6s, exhale 8s

Allow your thoughts

to just be there!

Where's your mind?

Bring it here!

Don't try to
change
your thoughts!

Breathe deeply

and slowly!

Notice your emotion

and let it be!

If your mind wanders 100 times

100 times
refocus it here!

It's normal for your

mind to wander!

The goal isn't to
make it perfect!

Nothing is perfect
and is alright!

Let your mind

chatter in the background

Let your thoughts

come, stay and go!

Notice how your

mind hooks you!

Allow your feelings

to be as they are!

Fix your attention

on this mandala!

Keep your attention 
on your breath!

If frustration arise

focus on the breath

If impatience arise

simply refocus here!

What's your mind
telling you now?

Imagine yourself

radiating kindness!

Take a minute to

breath deeply!

Allow yourself to

be nice to yourself!

Focus on one thing
and keep going!

Bring back
your attention!

It's ok to

feel sad!

Think about the

good things of today

Breathe deeply and

notice how you
relax

Bring to mind a

helpful story!

Little things are

beautiful too!

Notice what
hooks you!

Let your mind
wander just a minute

Put away your

hooking thoughts!

Make your life

MEANINGFULL

Thanks
for being
here